Where Does It Come From?

From Sheep to Sock

by Avery Toolen

Bullfrog Books

Ideas for Parents and Teachers

Bullfrog Books let children practice reading informational text at the earliest reading levels. Repetition, familiar words, and photo labels support early readers.

Before Reading

- Discuss the cover photo. What does it tell them?

- Look at the picture glossary together. Read and discuss the words.

Read the Book

- "Walk" through the book and look at the photos. Let the child ask questions. Point out the photo labels.

- Read the book to the child, or have him or her read independently.

After Reading

- Prompt the child to think more. Ask: What kind of socks do you wear? Have you ever thought about where they come from?

Bullfrog Books are published by Jump!
5357 Penn Avenue South
Minneapolis, MN 55419
www.jumplibrary.com

Library of Congress Cataloging-in-Publication Data

Names: Toolen, Avery, author.
Title: From sheep to sock / by Avery Toolen.
Description: Minneapolis, MN: Jump!, Inc., [2022]
Series: Where does it come from? | Includes index.
Audience: Ages 5–8. | Audience: Grades K–1.
Identifiers: LCCN 2020047827 (print)
LCCN 2020047828 (ebook)
ISBN 9781645279822 (hardcover)
ISBN 9781645279839 (paperback)
ISBN 9781645279846 (ebook)
Subjects: LCSH: Woolen goods—Juvenile literature.
Socks—Juvenile literature. | Wool—Juvenile literature.
Classification: LCC TS1626 .T66 2022 (print)
LCC TS1626 (ebook) | DDC 338.4/76773—dc23
LC record available at https://lccn.loc.gov/2020047827
LC ebook record available at https://lccn.loc.gov/2020047828

Editor: Eliza Leahy
Designer: Michelle Sonnek

Photo Credits: valkoinen/Shutterstock, cover (left); Eric Isselee/Shutterstock, cover (right), 1; PeJo/Shutterstock, 3; GrashAlex/Shutterstock, 4; patjo/Shutterstock, 5, 23tl; Juice Flair/Shutterstock, 6–7, 22tl, 23bm; James King-Holmes/Alamy, 8–9; iStock, 10, 22tr; Sergieviev/Shutterstock, 11; wpohldesign/iStock, 12–13, 22mr, 23tm; Science & Society Picture Library/Getty, 14–15, 22br, 23tr; Bloomberg/Getty, 16; JIANG HONGYAN/Shutterstock, 17, 22bl, 23bl; Lee waranyu/Shutterstock, 18–19; DisobeyArt/Shutterstock, 20–21, 22ml; Reinhold Leitner/Shutterstock, 23br; Evikka/Shutterstock, 24.

Printed in the United States of America at Corporate Graphics in North Mankato, Minnesota.

Table of Contents

Spin and Knit

Hank wears wool socks.

Where do they come from?

Sheep!
Their coats are made of wool.

wool

Farmers shear sheep.

wool

The wool goes to a factory.

It is washed.

A machine smooths it.

Another machine spins it.

yarn

This makes yarn.

Yarn is dyed.

It comes in many colors.

Fun!

yarn

A machine knits
each sock.

It takes a
few minutes.

Wow!

Socks are washed
and dried.

They are paired.

Socks are sent to stores.

We buy them!

Our feet stay warm!

From Wool to Feet

How is sheep wool made into socks we wear? Take a look!

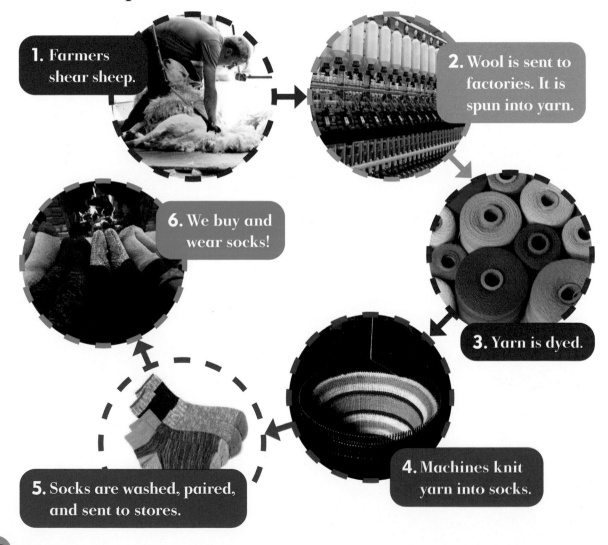

1. Farmers shear sheep.

2. Wool is sent to factories. It is spun into yarn.

3. Yarn is dyed.

4. Machines knit yarn into socks.

5. Socks are washed, paired, and sent to stores.

6. We buy and wear socks!

Picture Glossary

coats
Outer layers of fur, hair, or wool on animals.

dyed
Changed the color of something using a substance.

knits
Makes fabric or clothing out of yarn.

paired
Grouped into sets of two.

shear
To cut or clip the hair or wool from an animal.

wool
The soft, thick, curly hair of sheep and other animals.

Index

To Learn More

Finding more information is as easy as 1, 2, 3.

❶ Go to www.factsurfer.com

❷ Enter "fromsheeptosock" into the search box.

❸ Choose your book to see a list of websites.